D1520490

ARAM PUBLIC LIBRARY
DELAVAN, WI

FORENSIC SCIENCE INVESTIGATED

FORENSICS
AND MEDICINE

WRITTEN BY:
Rebecca Stefoff

mc Marshall Cavendish
Benchmark
New York

COPYRIGHT © 2011 MARSHALL CAVENDISH CORPORATION
Published by Marshall Cavendish Benchmark
An imprint of Marshall Cavendish Corporation
All rights reserved.

No part of this publication may be reproduced, stored in a retrieval system or transmitted, in any form or by any means, electronic, mechanical, photocopying, recording, or otherwise, without the prior permission of the copyright owner. Request for permission should be addressed to the Publisher, Marshall Cavendish Corporation, 99 White Plains Road, Tarrytown, NY 10591. Tel: (914) 332-8888, fax: (914) 332-1888. Website: www.marshallcavendish.us This publication represents the opinions and views of the author based on Rebecca Stefoff's personal experience, knowledge, and research. The information in this book serves as a general guide only. The author and publisher have used their best efforts in preparing this book and disclaim liability rising directly and indirectly from the use and application of this book. Other Marshall Cavendish Offices: Marshall Cavendish International (Asia) Private Limited, 1 New Industrial Road, Singapore 536196 • Marshall Cavendish International (Thailand) Co Ltd. 253 Asoke, 12th Flr, Sukhumvit 21 Road, Klongtoey Nua, Wattana, Bangkok 10110, Thailand • Marshall Cavendish (Malaysia) Sdn Bhd, Times Subang, Lot 46, Subang Hi-Tech Industrial Park, Batu Tiga, 40000 Shah Alam, Selangor Darul Ehsan, Malaysia Marshall Cavendish is a trademark of Times Publishing Limited

All websites were available and accurate when this book was sent to press.

LIBRARY OF CONGRESS CATALOGING-IN-PUBLICATION DATA
Stefoff, Rebecca
Forensics and medicine / by Rebecca Stefoff.
p. cm. — (Forensic science investigated)
Includes bibliographical references and index.
ISBN 978-0-7614-4143-4
1. Medical jurisprudence—Juvenile literature. 2. Forensic pathologists—
Juvenile literature. 3. Forensic pathology—Juvenile literature. I. Title.
RA1053.S67 2011
614'.1—dc22
2010010526

EDITOR: Christina Gardeski   PUBLISHER: Michelle Bisson
ART DIRECTOR: Anahid Hamparian   SERIES DESIGNER: Kristen Branch

Photo Research by Lindsay Aveilhe
Cover photo by doc-stock/Corbis
The photographs in this book are used with permission and through the courtesy of: Richard B. Levine/Newscom: p. 4; Massimo Petranzan/Alamy: p. 9; Photo Researchers: p. 12; John Barr/Liaison Agency/Getty Images: 15; Shepard Sherbell/Corbis SABA: p. 18; Photo Library: p. 21; Mauro Fermariello/Photo Researchers: p. 24; Joshua Lawton/Newscom: p. 27; Custom Medical Stock Photo: p. 31; Kallista Images/Getty Images: p. 34; Beatrice de Gea/The New York Times: p. 37; Najlah Feanny/Corbis SABA: 40; Charles Thatcher/Getty Images: p. 42; Depphotos/Newscom: p. 44; Zuma/Newscom: p. 47; Photo Researchers: p. 50; Yellow Dog Productions/Getty Images: p. 52; Photo Library: p. 59; Peter Dazeley/Getty Images: p. 60; Elaine Thompson/AP Photo: p. 63; Jetta Productions/Walter Hodges/Getty Images: p. 66; Photo Researchers: p. 68; David Longstreath/AP Photo: p. 71; Imagechina via AP Images: p. 74; Jon Way/Time Life Pictures/Getty Images: p. 77; FBI/AP Photo: p. 78; Photo Researchers: p. 81; USAMRIID/Handout/Reuters: p. 83.

Printed in Malaysia (T)
1 3 5 6 4 2

Cover: Techniques from the medical or chemistry lab can play a key role in criminal investigation.

CONTENTS

The international symbol for a biological hazard is a reminder that letters once spread a deadly disease.

WHAT IS FORENSICS?

WHEN PEOPLE GET SICK and die after opening letters sent through the U.S. mail. . . .

When a boy or girl is brought to a hospital emergency room with suspicious-looking bruises and burns. . . .

When desperate parents buy medicine for their sick children but get only a worthless counterfeit pill that cheats them of money and hope. . . .

In these cases and others, discovering the truth calls for a special combination of medical science and crime-solving techniques. That combination, known as forensic medicine, is one branch of **forensic science**.

Forensic science is the use of scientific methods and tools to investigate crimes and bring suspects to trial. The term "forensic" comes from ancient Rome, where people debated matters of law in a public meeting place called the Forum. The Latin word *forum* gave rise to *forensic*, meaning "relating to courts of law or to public debate."

Today the term **forensics** has several meanings. One is the art of speaking in debates, which is why some schools have forensics clubs or teams for students who want to learn debating skills. The best-known meaning of "forensics," though, is crime solving through **forensic science**.

Fascination with forensics explains the popularity of many TV shows, movies, and books, but crime and science have been linked for a long time. The first science used in criminal investigation was medicine, and one of the earliest reports of forensic medicine comes from ancient Rome. In 44 BCE, the Roman leader Julius Caesar was stabbed to death not far from the Forum. A physician named Antistius examined the body and found that Caesar had received twenty-three stab wounds, but only one wound was fatal.

Antistius had performed one of history's first recorded **postmortem** examinations, in which a physician looks at a body to find out how the person died. But forensics has always had limits. Antistius could point out the chest wound that had killed Caesar, but he could not say who had struck the deadly blow.

Death in its many forms inspired the first forensic manuals. The oldest one was published in China in 1248. Called *Hsi duan yu* (The Washing Away of Wrongs), it tells how the bodies of people who have been strangled differ from drowning victims. When a corpse is recovered from the water, says the manual, officers of the law should examine the tissues and small bones in the neck. Torn tissues and broken bones show that the victim met with foul play before being thrown into the water.

Poison became another landmark in the history of forensics in 1813, when Mathieu Orfila, a professor of medical and forensic chemistry at the University of Paris, published *Traité des poisons* (A Treatise on Poisons). Orfila described the deadly effects of various mineral, vegetable, and animal substances. He laid the foundation of the modern science of **toxicology**, the branch of forensics that deals with poisons, drugs, and their effects on the human body.

As France's most famous expert on poisons, Orfila played a part in an 1840 criminal trial that received wide publicity. A widow named Marie LaFarge was accused of poisoning her husband. Orfila testified that upon examining LaFarge's corpse he had found arsenic in the stomach. The widow insisted that she had not fed the arsenic to her husband, and that therefore he must have eaten it while away from home. The court, however, sentenced her to life imprisonment. Pardoned in 1850 after ten years in prison, LaFarge died the next year, claiming innocence to the end.

Cases such as the LaFarge trial highlighted the growing use of medical evidence in criminal investigations and trials. Courts were recognizing other kinds of forensic evidence, too. In 1784 a British murder case had been decided by physical evidence. The torn edge of a piece of newspaper found in the pocket of a suspect named John Toms matched the torn edge of a ball of paper found in the wound of a man who had been killed by a pistol shot to the head (at the time people used rolled pieces of cloth or paper, called wadding, to hold bullets firmly in gun barrels). Toms was declared guilty of murder. In 1835, an officer of Scotland Yard, Britain's famous police division, caught a murderer by using a flaw on the fatal bullet to trace the bullet to its maker. Such cases marked the birth of ballistics, the branch of forensics that deals with firearms.

Not all forensic developments involved murder. Science also helped solve crimes such as arson and forgery. By the early nineteenth century, chemists had developed the first tests to identify certain dyes used

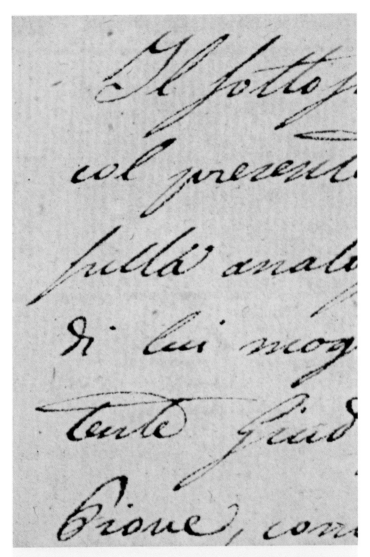

▲ Is this old Italian letter a genuine antique or a modern forgery? The chemical makeup of the ink may provide a clue to forensic document examiners.

in ink. Experts could then determine the age and chemical makeup of the ink on documents, such as wills and valuable manuscripts, that were suspected of being fakes.

Forensics started to become a regular part of police work at the end of the nineteenth century, after an Austrian law professor named Hans Gross published a two-volume handbook on the subject in 1893. Gross's book, usually referred to as *Criminal Investigation,* brought together all the many techniques that scientists and law enforcers had developed for examining the physical evidence of crime—bloodstains, bullets, and more. Police departments started using *Criminal Investigation* to train officers. The book entered law school courses as well.

Modern forensics specialists regard Hans Gross as the founder of their profession. Among other contributions, Gross invented the word "criminalistics." He used it to refer to the general study of crime or criminals. Today, however, criminalistics has a narrower, more specific meaning. It refers to the study of physical evidence from crime scenes. "Forensics" is a more general term. It covers a broader range of investigative techniques and activities, including many drawn from the field of medicine.

Toxicological testing, as in the LaFarge case, is just one technique that was developed by researchers in biology or medicine, then proved its value as a forensic tool. Other medical sciences that contribute to criminal investigation include **odontology**, the study of teeth and dental work; **serology**, the study of blood and other body fluids; and **taphonomy**, the study of how bodies change after death. The discovery of **DNA**, the material in all of our cells that contains our individual genetic codes, was a triumph of modern biology and medicine. That discovery also gave us **DNA typing**, a technique that police and detectives now use to identify unknown crime victims and to prove that suspects were at crime scenes.

Forensic nursing is a fairly new form of forensic medicine in which nurses interact with patients who may be crime victims. The primary job of a forensic nurse is to collect evidence that might become part of a criminal investigation or a trial. This type of forensic medicine focuses on helping or protecting people who are alive. Yet just as in the time of Antistius, the doctor who examined the body of murdered Julius Caesar, one of the most important tasks facing forensic medical experts is still the study of the dead.

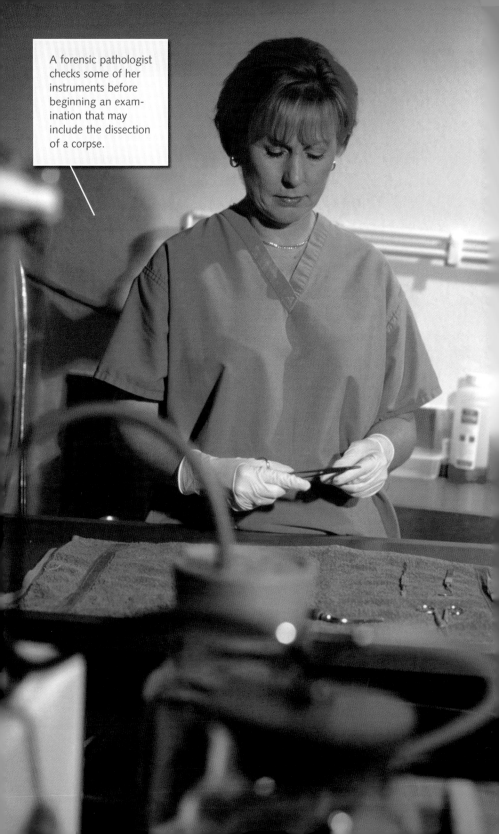

A forensic pathologist checks some of her instruments before beginning an examination that may include the dissection of a corpse.

CHAPTER ONE

DOCTORS
FOR THE DEAD

▼ **MOST PHYSICIANS CARE FOR THE LIVING,**

but sometimes the dead need medical experts, too.

Death is not usually mysterious. The majority of people die because of diseases or medical conditions that are known to the doctors who treated them, or for reasons that a doctor can easily identify, such as a fatal injury, heart attack, or infection. In such cases there is rarely a question about the cause of death.

Questions are asked, however, when someone dies suddenly and unexpectedly, or for no obvious reason, or in violent or suspicious circumstances. Authorities for the county or state want to know how that person died. For one thing, the cause of death is a necessary part of an official record called the death certificate. Even more important is finding out whether a crime was committed. For that reason, authorities need to know not just the cause of death but the manner of death. In other words, was the death natural, an accident, a suicide, or a **homicide**?

Figuring out the cause and manner of a death can be difficult. Take the case of a man who slips and falls while fishing from a rock jetty in an isolated part of the ocean coast. He is found dead two days later. Did the impact of falling off the jetty kill him at once? Or did he survive the fall but drown when the water covered him at high tide, or die of exposure in the cold and rain? Only a medical examination can determine the exact cause of his death.

What about the manner of the fisherman's death? Falling while fishing is not a natural death, but was the fall an accident? Had the man intended to commit suicide? Or was he murdered? Medical evidence might provide an answer here, too. Do the victim's medical records show a history of depression? Was he taking medication that could have affected his balance or his judgment? Are there cuts or bruises on his body that might have come from fighting off an attacker, or from being hit or pushed? Medical evidence—combined with other kinds of investigating, such as searching the man's home for a suicide note and questioning people who knew him—may tell the story.

▶ LEGAL AND MEDICAL ROLES

On average, about 80 percent of all deaths in the United States each year are easily explained. The other 20 percent come under investigation to determine the cause and

▲ Every death certificate must specify the cause of death. In the case of this twenty-year-old man, who died in Los Angeles in 1993, the cause of death was gunshot wounds.

manner of death. In most states, the law requires that all suspicious deaths, as well as all sudden and unexpected deaths, or deaths of people who were not under medical care, be investigated. This includes the deaths of infants, children, and teenagers. A young person's death is always investigated unless the cause of death is obvious.

Death investigations are sometimes called medicolegal investigations, which means that finding the cause and manner of death is both a medical matter and a legal responsibility. The state gives that responsibility to legal and medical professionals of various types. Depending upon the location and circumstances of a death, the official in charge of a death investigation may be a **coroner**, a **medical examiner (ME)**, or a **pathologist**.

CORONER

The office of coroner first appeared in England centuries ago. During the colonial period, English settlers brought the post of coroner, along with other English legal and administrative practices, to North America. The coroner was the member of the local or colonial government who determined whether a death was natural or criminal, for purposes of official record keeping and to identify cases that called for investigation.

After the United States became an independent nation and each state made its own rules for death investigation, all the states adopted the coroner system. As elected officials, usually representing individual counties, coroners were responsible for determining the manner and cause of death. A coroner did not have to be a physician, but coroners were generally expected to get advice and assistance from doctors whenever there was any doubt about how someone had died.

The coroner system remains in place today in some states. Occasionally the office of coroner is combined with that of county sheriff. In many places, however, the official in charge of death investigations is now required to be a medical professional. Some states have passed laws saying that coroners must be physicians. Most, however, have given responsibility for death investigation to a new official, the medical examiner.

MEDICAL EXAMINER

In 1877 Massachusetts became the first state to replace the office of coroner with that of medical examiner. Like a coroner, a medical examiner had the legal responsibility of determining cause and manner of death. Unlike a coroner, however, an ME was a licensed physician.

By the mid-twentieth century, a number of other states either had replaced coroners with medical examiners or had begun to require coroners to work with medical examiners. The switch from coroner to

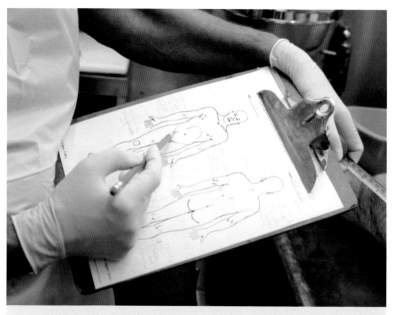

▲ A staff member in a medical examiner's office makes notes on an autopsy report. The subject of the autopsy can be seen on the examining table, lower right.

ME was sometimes brought about by public scandals. In the early twentieth century in New York City, for example, several people died during surgery because the anesthetic that was supposed to make them unconscious was wrongly applied. Afterward, New York State passed a law saying that whenever someone died during surgery, the death must be investigated by a medical examiner. In the 1960s , a series of newspaper articles in Allegheny County, Pennsylvania, exposed the short-comings of the coroner, a professional cabinetmaker with no medical background. The following year, the county's voters chose a new coroner—a physician.

Today voters in some states elect their county MEs. In many states, however, the MEs are appointed by state or county governments. A county may have a single medical examiner or, depending upon its size and needs, a chief medical examiner (CME) with a large staff of MEs. In some counties, the medical examiner is required to be a special type of physician called a forensic pathologist.

FORENSIC PATHOLOGIST

In the middle of the nineteenth century, doctors and medical researchers began using microscopes to examine the tumors and tissues that were removed from sick or dead hospital patients. This work developed into a medical specialty called pathology, which is the study of disease. By the middle of the twentieth century, pathologists were involved in legal and police work, helping coroners and medical examiners investigate deaths. Today that activity is known as forensic pathology. A forensic pathologist uses his or her special medical training to help determine the cause and manner of death. Often it is the forensic pathologist who proves that someone's death was the result of a crime—and this may keep a killer from getting away with murder.

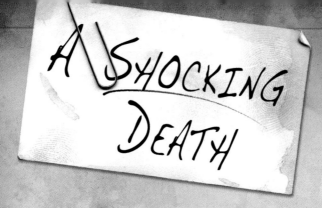

A SHOCKING DEATH

AFTER A THUNDERSTORM, a child was found dead in a bus shelter. The boy's mother had reported him missing just the day before, but already ants were nibbling at his body. The cause of death seemed to be electrocution—but this case, which was eventually investigated by forensic pathologist, doctor of law, and professor Ronald K. Wright, shows that when death is sudden and unexpected, medical findings may be tied to scientific and legal questions.

The dead boy was found lying on the ground with one leg touching a metal pipe that ran between a street light and the bus shelter. The purpose of the pipe, called a conduit, was to shield the wiring that carried electricity from a transformer on the light pole to the lights in the shelter.

The local forensic pathologist examined the boy's body at the scene, before it was moved. He saw that the leg touching the conduit had a mark that looked like a burn. Later, an autopsy showed that the discoloration *was* a burn. There was another burn on one knee, and something had burned all the way through one of the boy's sneakers to char the flesh of his foot. The autopsy also showed that the boy had not been suffering from any disease or illness at the time of his death. The pathologist decided that the boy had been killed by a low-voltage electrical current. But how?

Investigators found that the companies that built the shelter had not gotten a permit from the city's building

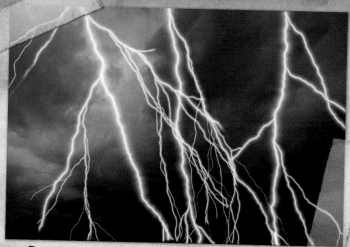

ELECTRICITY CAN BE FATAL, ESPECIALLY WHEN IT STRIKES FROM THE SKY.

department, which sets standards for all types of construction. They also discovered that the transformer on the light pole had a flaw, or short, in its insulation. The short had let an electrical current leak into the conduit. Even the metal bench inside the bus shelter had a small amount of current—about 40 volts—flowing through it.

The city filed charges against the builders of the shelter, who hired Wright to examine the facts in the case. Wright studied the autopsy results and the reports from the scene of death, and he found that the facts didn't add up. The wiring at the site could not have carried more than 480 volts of electricity—yet it would have taken thousands of volts to cause the flaw in the transformer's insulation and to burn through the boy's rubber sneaker.

Pointing out that death had occurred during a thunderstorm, Wright said that the boy had been electrocuted by lightning, not by a faulty electrical installation. A bolt of lightning had shorted out the transformer, and the sudden jolt of electricity traveling through the conduit had burned through the boy's shoe, killing him. The other burns had occurred after death, when his body was lying on the conduit. The puzzle of the child's tragic death was solved.

Anyone who wants to become a forensic pathologist must be prepared for years of study, beginning with a four-year college or university program. The next step is to become a physician by graduating from a four-year medical school and passing a state certifying exam. After medical school comes another four years of training, to specialize in pathology. This training usually takes the form of a medical residency, which gives the doctor on-the-job experience in a hospital. An additional year or two of training in the office of a coroner or ME focuses on forensic pathology. After completing all this training, the candidate takes a written test that may last for several days. A candidate who passes this examination becomes a certified forensic pathologist.

Many forensic pathologists work in medical examiners' or coroners' offices. Others work in hospitals or private practice, or teach in universities. Pathologists who do not work as full-time MEs may occasionally serve as consultants, lending their knowledge and skills to law enforcement agencies that either don't have a full-time ME or need additional expert help with a challenging case. Attorneys may also ask forensic pathologists to serve as witnesses in court. A forensic pathologist may be asked to supply expert testimony either for the prosecution (the state) or for the defendant (the person charged with the crime).

▶ POSTMORTEM PROCEDURES

The term *postmortem* means "after death." Anything that happens to a person's body after death is a postmortem event. A pathologist can tell, for example, whether a fatal stab wound took place postmortem or **antemortem**, which means "before death." This information can be vital to figuring out exactly what happened to the victim.

When someone dies as a result of a crime or an accident, an ME or a forensic pathologist examines the body. That examination, which is sometimes called a postmortem, involves collecting information from the body itself, from the scene of death, and from medical and other records.

THE CRIME SCENE
AND THE CHAIN OF CUSTODY

When a crime occurs, or is suspected, the first to arrive may be police officers, sheriff's deputies, firefighters, or others who answer emergency calls. These first responders share the same top priority, which is saving lives and keeping people safe. The second priority is processing the crime scene, which is the responsibility of the local law enforcement authority. Crime scene work is usually carried out by officers with special training in forensics. They may be called criminalists, crime scene investigators, evidence technicians, or scene-of-crime officers.

Processing a crime scene involves several steps. The first step is to secure the crime scene, which means keeping unauthorized people from entering the area and possibly destroying evidence. The second step is to record the scene in detail—with photographs, measurements, sketches, and possibly video—before anything is moved. The third step is to locate and collect all evidence, from fingerprints to bodies.

Crime scene processing must be done according to an important forensic principle called the **chain of custody**. The purpose of the chain of custody is to account for

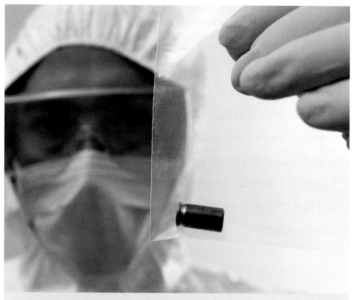

▲ Careful not to contaminate the evidence, a forensic officer collects a cartridge case found at a murder scene.

each piece of evidence from the time it is collected all the way to the moment it is produced in court.

A chain of custody is simply a list of everyone who has had contact with the evidence. Every person who handles or examines the evidence must sign the evidence container and note the date and time. Before an individual turns over the evidence to someone else, he or she must get the signature of the person, who becomes part of the chain. The goal is to have an unbroken chain of custody, or responsibility, for each piece of evidence. If the chain of custody is incomplete or broken, the evidence may prove worthless in court. A lawyer could argue that someone unknown had a chance to tamper with the evidence during any unaccounted-for period of time.

The requirement to maintain the chain of custody applies to all the evidence that forensic medical specialists examine, whether the item is as large as a body or as small as a few skin cells sent to a lab for DNA analysis. Many medical examiners' labs now use computerized tracking systems to record the chain of custody for each piece of evidence.

INITIAL EXAMINATION OF THE BODY

For a forensic pathologist or other medical expert called to examine a crime victim, the first step is an overall survey of the body. In ideal circumstances, a medical expert has the chance to look at the body just as it was found, before it is moved. Medical examiners and pathologists sometimes go to crime or accident scenes, but this is not always possible. Instead of seeing the crime scene in person, the forensic medical expert may rely on photographs, videos, or sketches made by the criminalists who collected evidence at the scene.

The body is removed from the scene of death and taken to the **morgue**, which is a specialized laboratory in a hospital or a forensic department. A morgue is a facility where bodies can be stored, studied, and dissected. Modern morgues are equipped with refrigerated storage lockers, dissecting tables, and an array of microscopes and medical tools. Cameras and video cameras are also standard equipment in morgues today, because all procedures there are thoroughly recorded.

If the medical expert has not gone to the scene, his or her first look at the body will be in the morgue. At this initial examination, the expert may be part of a postmortem team. Other members might include pathology assistants, a photographer or videographer to document each stage of the proceedings, a police officer or detective, and criminalists or forensic technicians who will take charge of any trace evidence, such as carpet fibers, hair, plant pollen, or broken glass, that is found on the victim's clothing or body. The clothing is evidence, too. Bloodstains or tears on the victim's clothes can help the team create a detailed picture of the death, while fingerprints, hair, or DNA found on the victim's clothing or possessions may be clues to the identity of another person who was present at the time of death—possibly a murderer.

The purpose of a postmortem is to discover how someone died—and, if the person was murdered, to recover any clues that might lead to the killer. The team looks for signs of trauma, or injury, such as cuts, broken bones, and gunshot wounds. All visible injuries are photographed and the damaged area carefully measured. The details of a stab wound or a crushed

▲ A coroner and medical investigator prepare to examine the outside of a body—the clothing and skin—as the first step in a death investigation.

skull may let a criminalist identify the type of weapon that was used, and that information may lead investigators to the attacker.

Some kinds of injuries are called defensive wounds because they are often seen on victims who have tried to protect themselves from attack. Broken fingers or gashes on the hands, for example, suggest that the victim's death was a homicide, not an accident or suicide.

Medical treatment can also leave signs of trauma on a victim's body. Emergency medical technicians, police, firefighters, or others who were first on the scene may have used cardiopulmonary resuscitation (CPR) or other first-aid techniques to try to revive the victim. Such techniques may cause injury—CPR can result in bruises or even broken ribs, for example. Separating treatment-related trauma from other injuries is an important part of the postmortem examination.

During the initial exam the medical expert removes scrapings from beneath the victim's fingernails and takes a sample of the victim's hair and blood. These samples from the victim can be compared with blood, body fluids, or other trace evidence found on the body or at the scene. Those comparisons, in turn, will reveal whether hairs or blood droplets, for example, came from another person, who may be viewed as a suspect if a crime was committed.

The postmortem team handles each piece of evidence with sterile gloves and immediately places it in a sealed container to keep it from being contaminated by stray hairs, dust, or other material circulating in the morgue. All evidence is labeled at once and handled according to the rules for keeping a proper chain of custody.

The last step in the initial examination is to wash the body and survey it again. This time the team looks for signs of trauma that might have been covered in blood or hidden by the victim's clothing. Bruises, bites, and smaller signs such as the pinprick injections of a hypodermic needle may now become visible. Finally, if the victim's identity is a mystery, the postmortem team records all distinctive features, such as tattoos or scars, along with height, weight, and fingerprints. These details may help investigators discover the identity of the **decedent**, or dead person.

RECORD REVIEW

If the decedent's medical records are available, the forensic pathologist or ME reviews them as early in the postmortem process as possible. Knowing that someone had a particular illness or disease can help the medical examiner pinpoint the cause of death. It is also important to learn what medications had been prescribed for the decedent. When the members of the forensic team know which drugs belonged in the decedent's bloodstream or tissues, they can focus on other drugs that may be evidence of accident, suicide, or homicide.

AUTOPSY

A death investigation may consist of nothing more than a review of medical records and a postmortem exam. If the cause of death is still unknown, however, or if foul play is suspected, the next step is an autopsy, or dissection of the body. The autopsy is performed in the morgue by a medical examiner or pathologist.

The examiner begins by using a knife or bone saw to make several large incisions, or cuts, to open the body. The result will be either a T-shaped incision, with one cut from shoulder to shoulder and another down the middle of the chest and abdomen, or a Y-shaped incision—today the T-shaped incision is more common. Either method lets the examiner fold back the skin and remove the stomach, lungs, heart, intestines, and other organs. Dissecting these organs will reveal information about the decedent's last meal and general state of health, as well as clues indicating certain kinds of disease or trauma.

The next step is to open the skull. The examiner first makes an incision across the top of the forehead,

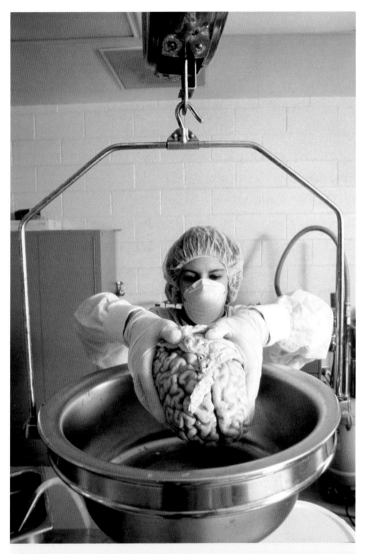

▲ During an autopsy, the brain is removed, weighed, and dissected or preserved for study. The examiner will take out other organs as well.

from ear to ear, and then peels away the scalp. Using a skull saw, the examiner removes the top of the skull and takes out the brain, which can then be examined for signs of trauma, such as a blow to the head, or of medical conditions, such as stroke or Alzheimer's disease. The brain is either dissected at once or stored in formaldehyde, a preservative that hardens the tissue and prevents **decomposition**.

The examiner may make other incisions in the decedent's back, arms, legs, hands, or feet to search for bruising beneath the skin. This is especially important when there is suspicion of multiple beatings or of torture. In addition, samples of the decedent's tissues, organs, and blood may be sent to other medical experts for specialized tests. The purpose of these tests may be to look for evidence of natural causes of death, such as disease or a blood clot that could have caused a stroke. The ME or forensic pathologist may also request toxicological screening, in which blood, urine, or tissue from the victim is tested for the presence of drugs or poisons.

A traditional autopsy involves significant damage to the body. For this reason, the dead person's relatives may not want the authorities to undertake the procedure. Religious belief is another reason people may cite for not wanting an autopsy to be performed. Followers of certain forms of the Jewish and Muslim faiths, for example, think that a body should be kept whole and not damaged after death. In cases of suspicious deaths, or deaths that may involve a public health emergency such as a contagious disease, however, authorities sometimes overrule a family's objections and perform an autopsy.

Law enforcement and public health agencies often meet with representatives of local religious communities to find ways to perform necessary postmortem procedures while showing respect for people's beliefs. Sometimes a limited or partial autopsy is all that is needed. In other cases, the forensic medical expert can get the necessary information without cutting into the body or taking samples from it. Instead of a traditional autopsy, the medical examiner performs a virtual autopsy.

A virtual autopsy involves scanners and screens rather than scalpels and saws. In a virtual autopsy, machines such as computed tomography (CT) scanners and magnetic resonance imagers (MRIs) allow death investigators to see inside a body without opening it. These devices can substitute for a traditional autopsy in some cases of sudden or unexplained death, but they cannot answer all questions. For example, a virtual autopsy can find bullets inside a body or reveal damage to bones and internal tissues, but it is no substitute for a detailed microscopic examination.

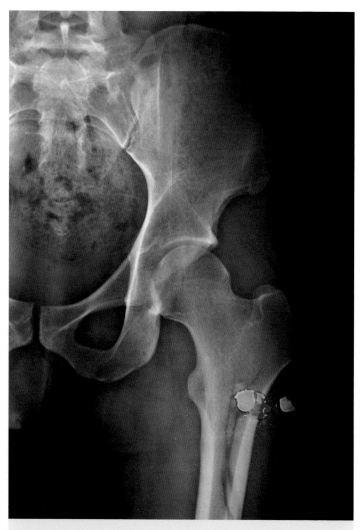

▲ Some traumas can be revealed without dissection. This X ray is a type of "virtual autopsy," showing fragments of the bullet that fractured the victim's thighbone.

The full traditional autopsy is still the forensic standard in criminal investigations.

Even when the cause of death seems obvious at first, an autopsy can reveal the unexpected. That's what happened in the case of Sandra Duyst, a woman who died of a gunshot wound to the head in her bedroom in Grand Rapids, Michigan, in 2000. Her husband, David Duyst, told police that he had been asleep in another room when the sound of a shot woke him. He found Sandra dead on the bed, with a gun lying next to her. He said that she had committed suicide because she was depressed.

The results of the initial postmortem exam fit the picture of suicide. The gun barrel had been pressed to Sandra's head, which is normal for gunshot suicides. There appeared to be a single entry wound, made by the bullet as it entered her skull on the right side, between her eye and her ear. There were two exit wounds on the left side of the skull, but that could have been caused by the bullet separating into two pieces after entry. Stephen D. Cohle, the forensic pathologist who examined Sandra's body, thought it was unusual that there was no blood on Sandra's hands, even though the gun and the bedsheets were bloody.

During the autopsy, the examiners shaved Sandra's head in preparation for opening her skull.

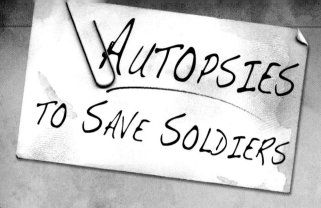

AUTOPSIES TO SAVE SOLDIERS

TWENTY-FIRST-CENTURY American soldiers who die in combat receive something new: full death investigations when their bodies come home. Beginning in 2001, when the United States went to war in Afghanistan, the Armed Forces Medical Examiner System has performed autopsies on the corpses of all servicemen and servicewomen killed on duty in Afghanistan and Iraq. The procedures take place in a special forensic pathology laboratory and morgue at Dover Air Force Base in Delaware, which is where the bodies of all overseas military fatalities are shipped.

Since 2004 the service people's bodies have also received computed tomography (CT) scans. A CT scanner uses a set of X-ray images to map the structures and features inside a body, producing a picture of the interior. This information helps the military medical examiners perform autopsies more quickly and efficiently. CT scans are especially good at showing the location in a body of any metal, such as a bullet or piece of shrapnel from an exploded bomb. The Armed Forces Medical Examiner System now has a database of more than three thousand scans of military injuries, the largest such collection in the world.

The autopsies and scans are authorized under federal law. They were started by Captain Craig T. Mallak, head of the Armed Forces Medical Examiner System, in order to give the families of military men and women full and accurate information about their loved ones' deaths. Families are notified of the autopsies, and between 85 and 90 percent of them ask to receive a copy of the autopsy report. What most families want to know, according to Mallak, is whether their loved one suffered. "If we can say, 'No, it was instantaneous, he or she never knew what happened,' they do get a great sense of relief out of that," says Mallak. "But we don't lie."

CAPTAIN CRAIG T. MALLAK SAW THE NEED TO CONDUCT AUTOPSIES ON ALL SERVICE PEOPLE KILLED IN AFGHANISTAN AND IRAQ.

The death investigations serve another purpose as well. They are revealing new ways to save the lives of military personnel. A study of one hundred of the CT scans showed that the chest walls of fallen soldiers are thicker now than they used to be, because soldiers, on average, are bigger and stronger. Because of this discovery, a piece of equipment in the kits of combat medics—a needle and tube for inflating a collapsed lung—was doubled in size to make sure that it can reach an injured soldier's lung.

Another finding from the Dover autopsies was that many deaths were caused by injuries that could have been prevented if body armor covered more of soldiers' shoulders and upper bodies. This discovery made headlines in 2006, leading to demands for more and better body armor for U.S. service people in combat zones. The bullets and bits of shrapnel that the medical examiners have recovered from soldier's bodies, especially since the CT scans began, are a source of information for the American military experts who analyze enemy weapons. In these ways and more, the knowledge gained by examining America's war dead has helped protect the nation's soldiers.

The pathology assistant discovered a second entrance wound that had been hidden by her hair. This meant that Sandra had received not one but two shots into her brain. But Cohle was certain that after the first shot Sandra would have been unable to move, much less fire a second shot. Suddenly, her death no longer looked like suicide.

The local sheriff's department took a closer look at David Duyst. They discovered that he was having an affair with another woman and was also experiencing financial problems. Sandra's life insurance would pay David more than half a million dollars, even if she committed suicide. This gave Duyst a motive for murder. Investigators began probing his story. They tested the shirt he had worn on the night of his wife's death and found tiny spots of her blood, which they said could have been sprayed onto the shirt when the bullet entered the victim's body.

Duyst insisted that he was innocent, but he was arrested and tried for the murder of his wife. The defense attorneys argued that the droplets of Sandra's blood had been sprayed onto on Duyst's shirt when he bent over Sandra's dying body, trying to help her, and she coughed. The defense team also suggested that a muscle reflex or twitch could have caused Sandra to fire two shots into her own head. Another theory about the two shots was that something could have gone wrong with the gun, making it fire twice even if Sandra pulled the trigger just once. The jury, however, was not convinced by these arguments. Jurors placed more weight on pathologist Cohle's statement that Sandra could not have fired the second shot. They found Duyst guilty of murder, although he continues to proclaim his innocence from behind bars.

EXHUMATION

Autopsies are usually performed soon after death. In some cases, though, an autopsy takes place years later. If a body has been buried and doubt later arises about the cause of death, a court may issue an order for exhumation, which is the opening of a grave to remove the body so that a forensic pathologist can autopsy it.

Depending upon the methods used to treat the body before burial, and the amount of time since burial, the autopsy may be less helpful than a procedure performed right after death would have been. Still, the presence of certain drugs in the dead person's tissue, or a tell-tale arrangement of broken bones, may show that a person everyone thought had died a natural death was really murdered.

Most exhumations take place because authorities have grown suspicious about a pattern of deaths.

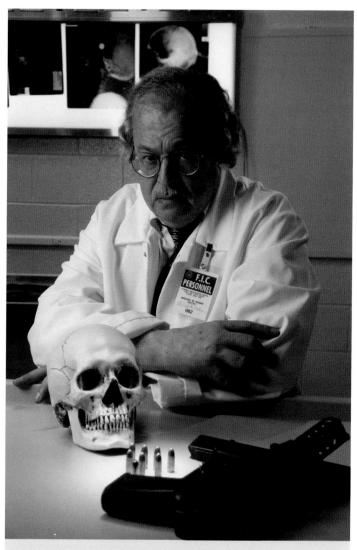

▲ A forensic doctor for New York's police displays the evidence of a crime: a semiautomatic gun and 9-millimeter bullets, a skull, and X rays showing the bullet hole in the bone.

"When the first baby suffocates or the first wife is poisoned, you don't know that," says Michael Baden, a New York pathologist and medical examiner. Those deaths may be accepted as due to natural causes or accidents. But if another such death occurs in the same family, authorities might decide to reopen those earlier cases—and graves. In cases of murder that have gone unsuspected for years or even decades, an exhumation followed by an autopsy can bring justice for the victims at long last.

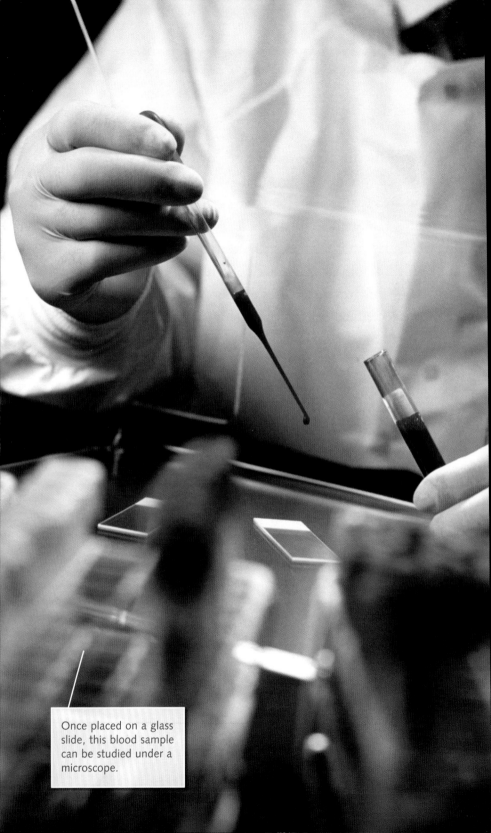

Once placed on a glass slide, this blood sample can be studied under a microscope.

CHAPTER TWO

FORENSIC NURSES AND SCIENTIFIC SPECIALISTS

▼ PATHOLOGISTS ARE NOT THE ONLY members of the medical profession who work in forensics. Experts in other branches of medical science also help in criminal investigations. They provide knowledge and skills in cases that range from tracking the makers of illegal drugs to finding a serial killer through bite marks left on his victims' bodies. Another area of forensic medicine involves nurses. Unlike pathologists, forensic nurses don't always work with corpses. Many of them use a combination of medical training and forensic procedures to aid the living.

▶ FORENSIC NURSING

Forensic nursing is the use of forensic principles or techniques by nurses. It is a fairly new field within both forensics and medicine in the United States. In 1991 the American Academy of Forensic Sciences recognized forensic nursing as a specialty. The American Nurses Association recognized the specialty in 1995. Forensic nurses have also established their own professional organization, the International Association of Forensic Nurses.

▲ Forensic nursing, which focuses on collecting evidence from living patients, is a new but important part of forensic medicine.

A forensic nurse is a registered nurse who, after receiving an education in nursing and passing a certification exam, has also received training in elements of forensic science, such as collecting evidence at a crime scene or providing expert testimony in court. One role for forensic nurses is death investigation. A forensic nurse may work in the morgue as part of a postmortem team or out in the field on a disaster recovery team, which works to identify the bodies of people killed in mass disasters such as hurricanes or airplane crashes. Many nurses, however, are part of a new direction in forensic science that is called living forensics. In living forensics, the focus isn't on corpses and morgues. It is on live people in hospital emergency rooms, medical clinics, and doctors' offices.

The idea behind living forensics is that the medical professionals who interact with crime victims can also support the goals of law enforcement and the justice system. Living forensics has two goals. One goal is to identify patients who have been harmed or who are at risk—such as victims of child abuse—so that they can be helped and protected from further harm. The other goal is to collect the evidence necessary to bring criminal charges against those who have done the harm.

Many nurses who work in living forensics are sexual assault nurse examiners (SANEs). They are nurses who have received special training in how to collect evidence in cases of rape and other forms of sexual assault. People who arrive at hospitals or doctors' offices after being sexually assaulted may be in urgent need of physical and emotional care. It is also important that evidence of the assault be properly collected, however, because it will be needed in court if the attacker stands trial.

A SANE knows how to conduct a forensic examination of the victim before evidence is washed away or lost. During the exam, the SANE not only notes and photographs all injuries but collects physical evidence such as hairs and body fluids from the victim's body and clothing. Because such an examination can be difficult for a person who is already suffering from the shock and pain of an attack, a SANE must have good communication skills. It is important to tell sexual assault victims, calmly and in a reassuring way, what is being done and why.

A sexual assault nurse examiner may recommend physical and psychological treatment for the victim, but the SANE does not provide care for the victim after the initial examination. That is because if a sexual assault nurse examiner became too closely involved with a victim, the nurse's evidence could be challenged in court as being tilted in the victim's favor. The same thing is true in all cases of suspected abuse, whether the victim is a child, a spouse, or an elderly person. If at all possible, the evidence should be collected or recorded by a trained forensic nurse, not by the nurse who is going to provide care and treatment to the patient. Like criminalists and pathologists, forensic nurses must know and follow the proper procedures for handling evidence, including the maintenance of a proper chain of custody.

▲ Elaine Pagliaro (left) and Barbara Moynihan wrote this textbook on forensic nursing, a growing medical specialty. A forensic nurse's activities may range from helping with a homicide investigation to testifying in court about child or elder abuse.

Forensic nurses may find themselves working with victims of appalling cruelty—victims who may be too young, too traumatized, or too mentally disturbed to speak for themselves. Many nurses, including forensic nurses, feel a passionate desire to help and care for such victims. Challenging though it is, forensic nurses must remain balanced and neutral, and they must not take sides. Their job is not to aid and comfort victims—others will do that. What forensic nurses do is make sure that evidence meets all legal and scientific standards, so that investigators and the courts will be able to arrive at the truth.

▶ MEDICAL AND SCIENTIFIC SPECIALTIES

Certain branches of medical science are especially useful in forensics. Medical examiners, police, and other investigators regularly request help from experts in drugs and poisons, or blood and DNA, or teeth and dental work.

TOXICOLOGY

The study of drugs, poisons, and other harmful substances is part of medical research. When this knowledge is applied to legal matters, it is called forensic toxicology or forensic chemical analysis.

Toxicology focuses on the effects on the body of harmful substances. A forensic toxicologist's expert knowledge concerns how a person's blood and other tissues react to the presence of alcohol, illegal drugs, medicines, or poisons. The task of identifying an unknown substance, however, may be carried out not by a toxicologist but by an analytical chemist, a scientist whose specialty is testing materials in order to identify them. A toxicologist is likely to work in a hospital or university. Most drug testing in crime labs is done by analytical chemists or forensic technicians with special training in drug analysis.

Forensic toxicology or analytical chemistry is laboratory work. It consists of applying scientific tests to samples—a piece of a dead person's liver, a packet of white powder seized in a drug arrest, or a container of blood or urine—to see whether the samples contain drugs or **toxins**. There are four main uses for these tests.

DEATH INVESTIGATIONS. During a postmortem examination, a forensic toxicologist may examine samples of the decedent's blood or tissue to see whether drugs or poisons caused the death, or contributed to it. Today, death as a result of drug overdose is more common than death by poison. Poisonings do occur—many are accidents, but some are suicides or homicides. The toxic substances involved, however, are more likely to be dangerous household materials, such as rodent killer or antifreeze, than traditional poisoner's tools such as arsenic, strychnine, and cyanide.

CONTRABAND MATERIALS. A contraband substance or item is something that is illegal, such as prohibited drugs (or prescription medicines in the hands of anyone other than the person for whom they were prescribed). When police or Drug Enforcement Agency officers collect evidence that they believe is contraband, they send it to an analyst to be tested. To bring criminal charges against a heroin dealer, for example, the state must be able to prove that the material found in the

▲ Investigators use vials like these to test substances at crime scenes. Each vial contains crystals that change color when exposed to a particular illegal drug, such as marijuana, LSD, or cocaine.

dealer's possession was really heroin. Detailed chemical analysis can do more than find out whether a powder is or is not heroin, however. Testers can often identify a drug's "fingerprint"—that is, its exact chemical makeup, including trace elements and contaminants. This may help authorities connect many individual dealers to a single supplier, or trace a connection between different crimes that involved the same batch of drugs.

DRIVING WHILE INTOXICATED. One of the most common uses of drug analysis is testing to see whether someone who has been driving badly, or has been in a car accident, is under the influence of drugs. The most commonly abused drug in such cases is alcohol. Unlike drugs that are illegal in any amount, such as cocaine or methamphetamine, alcohol can legally be consumed by adults. In the United States, however, in every state and the District of Columbia, it is illegal to drive with a blood alcohol content (BAC) above 0.08 percent. In addition, some states have set lower limits for young drivers.

Police, state troopers, or sheriff's deputies can test a driver's breath at the scene of an accident or traffic stop using a device called a Breathalyzer, which estimates a person's BAC based on the amount of alcohol in his or her breath. The reading from a Breathalyzer is

▲ A police officer administers a breath test to see whether a driver has consumed too much alcohol to drive legally.

called a BrAC. Depending upon state laws and the type of machine used, the BrAC may be admitted as evidence in court. In some places, however, a blood test is required to prove intoxication over the legal limit.

WORKPLACE DRUG TESTING. Each year, toxicology and chemical laboratories perform hundreds of thousands of employment-related drug tests to find out whether people abuse illegal drugs such as marijuana, cocaine, or methamphetamine. Most tests are performed on urine samples because these can be collected without needles. Urine tests typically are part of the job application process. Because employers have learned that drug use is linked to higher rates of theft, accidents, absenteeism, and poor performance, a potential employee who fails a drug test probably will not get the job.

In some circumstances, the law permits testing of persons who have already been hired. If an employee's behavior suggests that he or she has been using alcohol or drugs on the job, a drug test may be required. And certain employees whose jobs involve public safety, such as police officers and airline pilots, can be tested at any time. Athletes in many sports must take drug tests to determine whether they have used steroids or other performance-enhancing substances that are banned by sports organizations.

TESTING FOR TOXINS

Analysts can test samples of many different kinds. For postmortem testing, blood is the most important sample because it gives the most accurate indication of toxins that may have been fatal. Ideally, a forensic toxicologist can get blood samples from two parts of the corpse: the heart and an arm or a leg. Postmortem exams should also include tests of the decedent's urine, because some toxins are more easily detected in urine than in blood.

Postmortem tests are sometimes done on other body parts, such as stomach contents. The material found in a decedent's stomach may show high concentrations of toxins, especially in cases of suicide. If someone dies very soon after swallowing sleeping pills or poison, for example, the toxin may not show up in the blood but will be present in the stomach. The liver, too, may show evidence of drugs or other toxins even if those substances are no longer present in the blood. Another tissue that can reveal drugs or toxins is the vitreous humor, the fluid inside the eye. When a corpse is so decomposed that no other samples are available, the eyes may remain relatively undecayed, giving toxicologists a liquid sample to test.

Hair can be tested for the presence of drugs, poisons, environmental toxins, or other chemical compounds. The disadvantage of using hair for chemical tests is that toxic substances are hard to detect because in most cases only tiny amounts of substances will be present in the hair. Another problem is that experts disagree about the reliability of such tests because substances can enter the hair shaft from the environment. Evidence of marijuana in someone's hair shaft, in other words, may mean that the person has been around marijuana smoke, not necessarily that he or she smoked it. The advantage of hair testing, however, is that many experts think that traces of drugs or poisons remain in hair forever. Experts may be able to estimate the dates of drug use from the way the drug is distributed along the hair shaft.

SEROLOGY

If you watch crime shows or follow the news, you know that DNA testing is a powerful tool in criminal investigation. Before there was DNA analysis, though, there was serology—the study of body fluids, especially blood. Serology still plays a role in forensics, although it has been somewhat overshadowed since the late 1980s by DNA analysis.

Serological tests include chemical procedures that fall into two groups: presumptive tests, also called screenings or screens, and confirmatory tests. A presumptive blood test is one that simply indicates whether blood is present. Such a test can reveal, for example,

A FATAL MISTAKE

WHEN A THIRTY-ONE-YEAR-OLD MAN collapsed and went into a coma during a fishing trip, his friends called for help. While they waited, the unconscious man's breathing grew fainter, and he turned blue in the face. Emergency medical help arrived too late—the man's heart stopped beating, and he could not be revived.

As usual in a case of sudden, unexpected death, an autopsy was held, but the autopsy did not reveal any sign of disease or trauma. What was the man's cause and manner of death? The answer was in the blood.

The medical examiner sent a sample of the fisherman's blood to a laboratory for toxicological testing. The lab found that the blood contained a narcotic drug called fentanyl. Although doctors prescribe this drug as a painkiller for cancer patients and others suffering from chronic pain, fentanyl is abused by people who obtain it illegally in order to get high. Too much fentanyl, however, is fatal. The dead man's blood contained 15 nanograms of fentanyl per milliliter, which is 25 percent more than the amount needed to kill a person. No wonder the man had died. But how had the fentanyl entered his system?

. . . . . .

· · · · ·

Investigators learned that the dead man had a history of drug abuse and that he had been employed by a funeral home. Not long before the fatal fishing trip, he had worked on the body of a woman who died of cancer. Before her death the woman had been using fentanyl patches, which sit on the surface of the skin and release the painkiller slowly into the system. Although the cancer patient's body had arrived at the funeral home bearing two fentanyl patches, these medical aids were later reported missing.

In attempting to reconstruct the incident, investigators theorized that the funeral home employee had removed the fentanyl patches from the woman's body. Instead of attaching them to his own skin, however, he may have soaked them and injected the fentanyl-containing liquid into his veins—but the drug was stronger than he expected. Instead of getting high, he died. His cause of death was fentanyl overdose. His manner of death was ruled an accident.

· · · · ·

whether a particular spot, stain, or puddle is blood or some other reddish substance. Most presumptive tests work by making blood change color or fluoresce (give off light). By performing these tests at a crime scene, criminalists can discover microscopic specks of blood between bathroom tiles that have been cleaned. Fluorescence testing can also reveal spots of blood on dark fabric, where it is not easily seen under normal light.

Presumptive tests indicate that certain stains do not need to be investigated, thus directing investigators to suspicious stains. But the tests do not prove absolutely that a given stain is human blood, nor do they identify its source. For those purposes, criminalists and serologists use confirmatory tests, which are specific and focused. The first step is to perform a presumptive test to determine whether a specimen is really blood. When the results are positive, other tests will be used to identify the species from which the blood came—is it human, or from a dog, cat, or other animal? If the specimen proves to be human, still more tests will be needed to determine the blood group and subtypes.

Every human being belongs to one of four large blood groups: A, B, O, and AB. A serological test can tell the blood group of a specimen. In addition, certain components of blood, such as enzymes and proteins, form recognizable subtypes that can be tested. Although tests

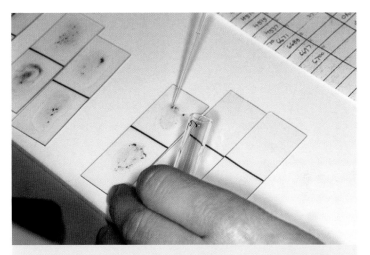

▲ Blood type or blood group testing has been part of medical science since the early twentieth century and remains a useful forensic tool.

for blood group and subtype cannot positively identify a blood specimen as coming from a particular person, they can show whether that person has the same blood group and subtypes as the specimen. This means that if a suspect's blood group and subtypes do not match those of the blood found under a murder victim's finger-nails, that suspect is not the person whom the victim scratched. But if the suspect's blood and the blood under the victim's nails belong to the same blood group and subtypes, investigators know only that the suspect *could* be the person scratched by the victim. The victim may have scratched someone else with that serological pro-file, or blood type.

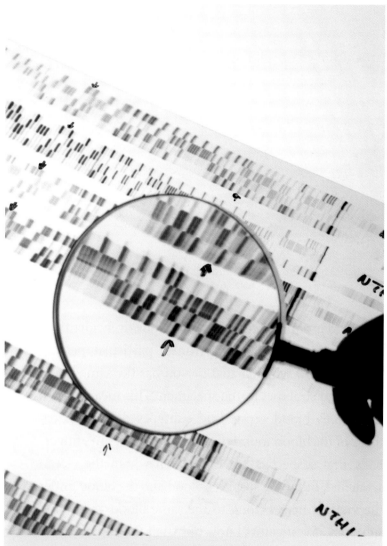

▲ The results of a DNA analysis look something like a bar code. Alternating dark and light blocks represent a person's unique genetic sequence.

DNA ANALYSIS

To prove a definite connection between a specimen and a source, forensic experts must move beyond serology to DNA analysis. Because DNA tests take longer and cost more than serological procedures, most investigations start with serology. The blood tests rule out the specimens that do not require DNA testing, so that investigators can focus on the specimens that may be important to the case. DNA analysis, however, is a complex and rapidly changing field. Not only are there many techniques for examining DNA, but new techniques are developed all the time.

DNA, or deoxyribonucleic acid, determines how the body's cells develop. It is the "blueprint" for every type of living organism, and it is also the means by which organisms pass on characteristics to their offspring.

All human cells contain two types of genetic material, mitochondrial DNA, or mtDNA, and nuclear DNA. Each human cell has thousands of copies of the mtDNA, located in structures called mitochondria. Both men and women inherit their mtDNA from their mothers. A person's mtDNA type is shared with his or her mother and with siblings from the same mother, but not with other relatives.

Nuclear DNA is contained in the center, or nucleus, of the cell. It exists in the form of chromosomes, which are long strands of molecules. These chromosomes are divided into units called genes, the building blocks of genetics. The nuclear DNA of every human being contains genes from two parents, arranged in a long pattern called a sequence. Every person's DNA sequence is individual and unique. Even identical twins have slight differences, called copy number variations, in their DNA profiles. An individual's DNA, however, is similar to that of his or her parents, siblings, and children. Victims of crimes or disasters can sometimes be identified by comparing DNA from the bodies with samples from close relatives.

The main forensic use of DNA analysis is in DNA typing, which uses an individual's DNA sequence as identification. Only a few individual humans have had their entire genetic sequences mapped—the process is currently extremely complex and expensive. For purposes of DNA typing, analysts attempt to compare sequences from thirteen loci, or positions, on the chromosomes. The odds of two people having the same DNA pattern in each of the thirteen loci are one in many billions, or even trillions. Not all DNA samples are created equal, however. Sometimes the available sample is too small to allow for a completely reliable DNA analysis. Other samples are found to be unusable because they have been too badly damaged by decomposition, heat, or chemicals.

▲ A specialist tests a shirt for DNA samples. In addition to new cases, labs are called on to analyze stored evidence from thousands of murders and rapes that took place years ago.

Mitochondrial DNA is much shorter than nuclear DNA, and it is less powerful for making identifications than nuclear DNA. However, usable mtDNA can sometimes be obtained from samples in which the nuclear DNA is too damaged to be analyzed.

DNA profiles can be obtained from blood, saliva, hair, or skin cells. They can be used to identify an unknown corpse or to link a criminal to a crime scene—but only if the forensic analyst is able to match the specimen from the corpse or the crime scene with an exemplar—that is, with a DNA profile of someone whose identity is known. A DNA sample cannot help investigators find a suspect among the general population unless that suspect's DNA profile is already on file. At this time, DNA databases in the United States contain only the profiles of convicted criminals and military personnel.

Although DNA typing cannot solve every crime, it is useful for ruling out some links between pieces of evidence and one or more suspects. If DNA evidence such as blood or other body tissue is available from the victim's body or the crime scene, that evidence can be compared with a suspect's DNA profile. If the two do not match, then that suspect did not leave the evidence (although that does not prove that the suspect was not involved in the crime).

In recent years hundreds of people imprisoned for crimes such as rape and assault have been freed because new tests have shown that their DNA does not match the DNA in evidence collected at the time of the crime. That is, it has now been shown that the evidence does not link them to the crimes for which they went to prison.

Methods of analyzing DNA are improving all the time. From the point of view of forensics, the most important goals are to make DNA analysis less expensive, easier to perform, and less time-consuming (analysis now takes at least several hours, and often days, weeks, or even longer because of the backlog at labs). Portable DNA analysis tools that can be used in the field, rather than in a special lab, are already being tested. Criminalists and law enforcement agencies look forward to the time when DNA tests are fast, available everywhere, and inexpensive enough to use in all cases.

ODONTOLOGY

Forensic odontology, also called forensic dentistry, is the use of dental science in legal matters. The focus is on teeth, but depending upon the type of investigation, the teeth may be those of a victim or those of a criminal.

Unknown victims—from nameless, decades-old skulls found in the woods to hundreds of bodies washed ashore after a tsunami—can often be identified by their teeth, if they received professional dental care during life. A forensic dentist or odontologist prepares a detailed description of the dead person's teeth, including any

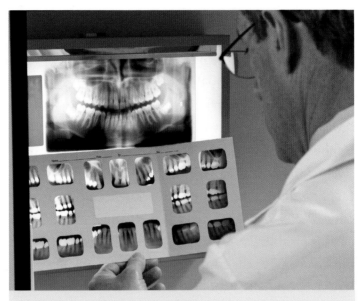

▲ A set of dental X rays is an effective way to identify an unknown victim of crime or disaster—if the victim received dental care while alive.

dental work such as fillings and false teeth, accompanied by photographs and X rays. If that description can be matched to the records kept by the victim's dentist, the remains have been identified. After a mass disaster such as an airplane crash, authorities try to gather the dental records of everyone who might possibly be involved. These records can be extremely helpful. They may be the most reliable way, or even the only way, to identify a body that has been badly burned or completely decomposed.

Dental identification can do more than identify victims. It may also help authorities link suspects to crimes.

Bite marks left in human tissue, for example, may be clues that point to a killer. In some cases, killers or attackers bite their victims, leaving imprints of their own upper and lower teeth. If a suspect's teeth match those imprints, that suspect may be the killer—or at least the biter. As evidence, however, bite marks are much less solid than dental records. For example, bruising or decay of the flesh may make bite marks difficult to measure precisely. In addition, unlike DNA profiles, bite marks are not unique. Many individuals have identical bite marks. A match between bite marks on a victim and a suspect's teeth may suggest a connection, but the match does not prove that the suspect bit the victim.

Crime victims who are fighting for their lives sometimes bite their attackers in self-defense. If a suspect's body shows defensive bite marks that match the victim's bite pattern, law enforcement officers will demand to know when and how the suspect was bitten.

Forensic dentistry does not always involve murder victims and bite marks. Dentists or odontologists may also be called as expert witnesses in cases of dental malpractice, when a dental patient claims that he or she received faulty or substandard dental care. The key to all aspects of forensic dentistry is a thorough knowledge of human dentition—the arrangement of teeth in a person's jaw—in all its variations.

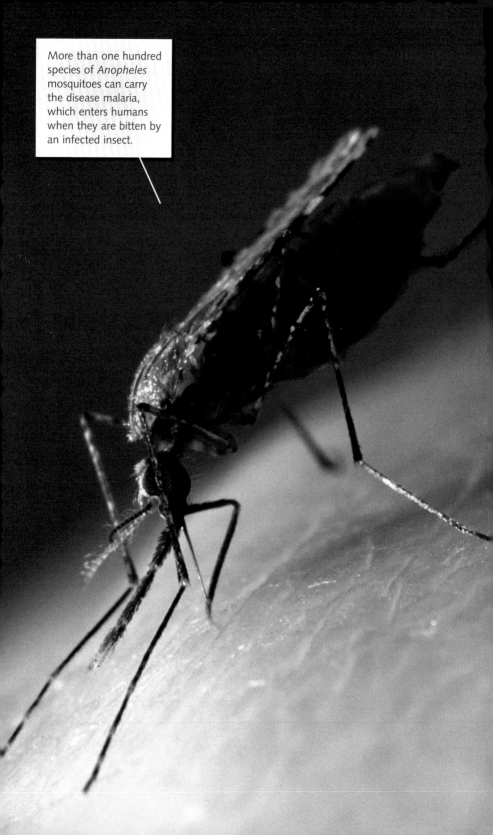

More than one hundred species of *Anopheles* mosquitoes can carry the disease malaria, which enters humans when they are bitten by an infected insect.

CHAPTER THREE

MEDICAL CRIMES

▼ **WHEN A CRIME INVOLVES DISEASE,**
solving it is a medical as well as a legal challenge. Two
criminal investigations, one in Southeast Asia and one
in the United States, show that fighting medical crime
requires the expert knowledge of law enforcement,
public health workers, doctors, and scientists.

▶ **CRACKING DOWN ON COUNTERFEIT MEDICINES**
Malaria is a disease caused by a parasite that is carried
by mosquitoes. The bite of an infected mosquito can
transmit the parasite into a human host, who then
becomes ill. In most cases, malaria can be cured by
early medical treatment. Without treatment, though,

malaria produces serious flu-like symptoms, including high fever and chills. It is sometimes fatal. The World Health Organization (WHO) estimates that there are 300 million to 500 million cases of malaria in the world each year, and 1 million deaths.

Malaria occurs in many parts of the world, but it is particularly severe and widespread in the tropics. In southeastern Asia, the disease is a major public health problem. Unfortunately, the very people who suffer from the disease are also at high risk of becoming victims of the crime of pharmaceutical counterfeiting, or the manufacture and sale of fake medicines.

Artesunate is one of Southeast Asia's most frequently used antimalarial medicines. In that part of the world, the majority of people do not go to hospitals or doctors' offices when they get sick. Many live far from such facilities or cannot afford them. Instead, people rely on drugstores or small village clinics for medical advice and treatment. People seeking relief from malaria probably buy a package of artesunate tablets from a local vendor. Since the late 1990s, however, a growing percentage of those pills have been fakes.

REAL OR FAKE?

In 1999 medical researchers bought artesunate from pharmacies in five southeastern Asian nations:

Vietnam, Laos, Cambodia, Thailand, and Myanmar (Burma). When the researchers analyzed the pills, they discovered that 38 percent of them were fakes. In a follow-up survey in 2003, an even higher proportion of pills—53 percent—were shown to be fake. One of the biggest makers of genuine artesunate, Guilin Pharmaceutical of China, had made its packaging more difficult to imitate—but the counterfeiters had managed to produce convincing fakes of the new packaging.

Malaria expert Nicholas White of Thailand called the counterfeiting of artesunate "a very, very serious

▲ Some people with malaria suffer a double blow. They buy medicine to treat the disease, but the pills they buy are worthless fakes.

criminal act." It was, he said, "premeditated, cold-blooded murder" because it robbed people of the medicine that might save their lives. In 2005 physicians, medical researchers, and public health officials met at WHO headquarters in the Philippines to discuss the artesunate crisis. They decided to work with the International Criminal Police Organization (Interpol), a law enforcement agency that deals with crimes involving multiple countries. Together Interpol and a team of medical and scientific experts would try to find and stop the artesunate counterfeiters. Interpol named the mission Operation Jupiter.

EXAMINING THE EVIDENCE

The first step was to obtain hundreds of samples of the fake pills. Operation Jupiter agents bought 391 packages of medicine, which were then analyzed at one of the laboratories of the Centers for Disease Control and Prevention in Atlanta. More than half the packages contained phony medicine. The 195 fakes were made of a surprising variety of ingredients: ordinary flour; several drugs that are known to cause cancer and are banned in the United States; a drug used to treat male impotence; trace amounts of antibiotics, which are useless against malaria; and acetaminophen, which relieves headache symptoms but does not treat malaria. One disturbing discovery was that many of the fakes contained trace amounts of artesunate—not enough to kill the malaria parasite, but perhaps enough to help the parasite develop a resistance to the drug. Not only would these counterfeit pills not cure malaria, but they might prevent people who took them from being helped, later, by genuine pills.

Experts in many fields examined everything from the printing on the fake packaging to tiny pollen grains that were found in the pills. The tablets contained pollen from a family of reeds that grows only along the coast of northern Vietnam and southern China. Combining that fact with other evidence, investigators concluded that the fake antimalarial medicine was being made somewhere in southern China. Two different networks of counterfeiters seemed to be responsible for manufacturing and distributing the fake drug.

A top Interpol official met in 2006 with a representative of the Chinese government and presented the findings of Operation Jupiter. It was now up to China to take action. After the Chinese Ministry of Public Security conducted its own investigation, its agents arrested one seller and two buyers for trafficking in counterfeit artesunate. Unfortunately, the makers of the fake pills were not found. Another operation in 2008, however, built on the work of Operation Jupiter to produce bigger results. Interpol, together with forensic

▲ Chinese police officers seized counterfeit drugs in a 2009 raid in Henan province, central China.

experts, physicians, and law enforcement agents from seven Asian countries, carried out two hundred raids that led to twenty-seven arrests. They also seized 16 million doses of counterfeit pharmaceuticals.

Still, the international trade in phony medicine continues to grow. One WHO report says that as many as a quarter of all medicines consumed in the world's developing nations may be bogus. A major battle in the war on counterfeit medications is the effort to trace the origin of fake malaria pills now being sold in Africa. Says Aline Plançon, head of Interpol's counterfeit drug crime division, "The more we work on these criminal networks, the more we see that they're interconnected across continents."

▶ AMERITHRAX

A 2001 medical crime—a case of anthrax poisoning through the U.S. mail—has been called "one of the largest and most complex [investigations] in the history of law enforcement." The Federal Bureau of Investigation (FBI) used that phrase to describe a case of biological terrorism that killed five people and made seventeen others ill. The case also tested a new tool called **microbial forensics**, with which investigators can now track the sources of the tiniest weapons ever used in mass crimes: deadly disease microbes.

The FBI called the case Amerithrax. The Amerithrax Task Force consisted of seventeen FBI agents and ten postal inspectors. They and other investigators conducted more than 9,100 interviews and 70 searches over a period of almost seven years. The case is still not officially closed, although the FBI believes that the person who committed the crime is dead.

ATTACK THROUGH THE MAIL

The case began on September 18, 2001, a week after the 9/11 terrorist attacks on New York City and Washington, D.C., had shocked the United States and the world. On that date, two letters were postmarked in Trenton, New Jersey. These letters were received by the New York City offices of the NBC broadcast network and the *New York Post*, a newspaper. The letters, which were not signed, contained a coarse, brown powder. People who had handled the letters fell ill. Authorities think that at least three other letters were mailed, because people in the New York City offices of the ABC and CBS networks, and in the Florida office of the *National Enquirer* newspaper, became ill with the same symptoms. If letters were sent to those locations, however, they were never found.

Three weeks later, letters postmarked in Trenton were sent to the Washington, D.C., offices of two

▲ Equipped with respirators and hazmat (hazardous materials) suits, Environmental Protection Agency officials search for disease spores after the 2001 anthrax attacks.

prominent Democratic politicians, Senator Tom Daschle of South Dakota and Senator Patrick Leahy of Vermont. These letters also contained powder, although in a slightly different form.

People who worked in the mail system or in the locations that received the letters were found to have anthrax, a deadly disease carried by bacterial spores that can travel through the air. Of the five people who died, one worked in the Florida newspaper office that

▲ This letter, containing anthrax spores, was mailed to Senator Patrick Leahy of Vermont. The disease is typically found in livestock but can be fatal to humans.

had received a letter postmarked September 18 and two worked in a mail-sorting facility in Washington. Authorities have never found out how the other two victims—a Vietnamese immigrant who worked in New York and an elderly woman who lived in Connecticut— were exposed to the anthrax spores.

The anthrax outbreak was quickly traced to the letters, which had contained at least two forms of anthrax material. A search of six hundred mailboxes in and around Trenton found only one with traces of anthrax powder. It was located in Princeton, New Jersey. By early 2002 the anthrax material had been identified with a strain of bacteria called the Ames strain, which had been the subject of research in an Army lab at Fort Detrick, Maryland, and a number of other U.S. locations. Still, the source of the letters remained a mystery.

THE SEARCH FOR THE SOURCE

In the weeks after the anthrax outbreak was recognized, some Americans feared a large-scale bioterrorist attack on the country. Many people, both in the government and among the general public, believed that the anthrax attacks had been carried out by the Islamic terrorist organization Al-Qaeda, the group responsible for the 9/11 attacks and other acts of terrorism around the world. No terrorist group claimed credit for the attacks, however, and investigators began to realize that the anthrax attacks might not be linked to known threats. The search was on for someone with access to anthrax materials who might have mailed the deadly letters.

Amerithrax investigators turned their attention to a research scientist named Steven Hatfill, who had worked at Fort Detrick and had written a report about the possibility of terrorists using anthrax in mail attacks. Although the FBI named Hatfill a "person of interest" in the case, he was never formally called a suspect. Not only has the FBI cleared Hatfill of involvement in the anthrax mailings, but he won $5.8 million in a lawsuit against the U.S. Justice Department for violating his privacy by giving his name to news reporters without any evidence he had committed a crime.

The real progress in the case took place in science labs. Researchers under contract to the U.S. government, as well as dozens of independent experts in microbiology (the study of bacteria) and other specialties, worked to sequence the anthrax DNA code and trace the specific material used in the attacks. The breakthrough came when researchers found that the attack anthrax had four distinctive genetic mutations, or changes, that set it apart slightly from the

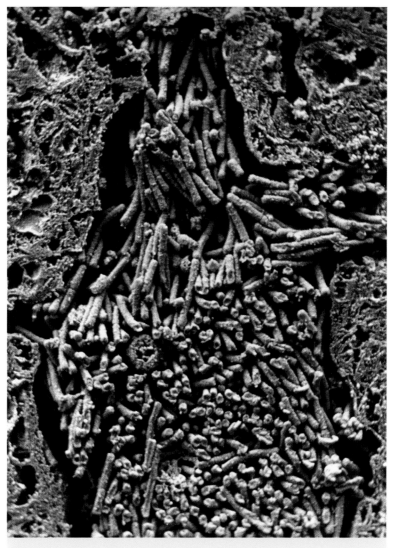

▲ Lung tissue infected with anthrax bacteria. Pulmonary anthrax, which attacks the lungs, is the most serious form of the disease.

basic genetic structure of the Ames anthrax strain. If investigators could find other samples of the Ames strain with the same mutations, they might find the source of the attack material.

The FBI collected a thousand samples from every facility known to have worked with the Ames anthrax strain. Researchers in the FBI laboratory examined those samples, comparing them to the material used in the anthrax attacks. Eight of the samples proved to have the same four mutations that had been found in the attack material. All eight of the samples were traced to a particular flask of anthrax spores developed at Fort Detrick. That flask was labeled RMR-1029. According to the FBI, it contained "the genetically unique parent material of the anthrax spores used in the mailings."

One hundred scientists had had access to the anthrax material in flask RMR-1029. After investigating all of them, the FBI focused on Bruce Ivins, a scientist who led research on anthrax vaccines at Fort Detrick and had created the spores in the fatal flask. By the summer of 2008, Ivins was the FBI's only serious suspect in the anthrax mailings. A few weeks after federal officials notified Ivins's lawyers that they felt they had a strong case against him, Ivins committed suicide. A U.S. district attorney declared that "Dr. Ivins was the only person responsible for these attacks." Yet his responsibility has never been proved, and many of those who have studied the case closely, including scientific experts in microbiology and bioweapons research, have doubts about his guilt.

▲ Scientist Bruce Ivins ended his life in 2008. The FBI thinks that he was the anthrax attacker, although his guilt has not been formally proven.

No evidence links Ivins to the letters or to the mailbox in Princeton. The case against him is based on his connection with RMR-1029 and the identification of RMR-1029 with the attack anthrax. In other words, the evidence in the case consists of highly technical scientific data based on new discoveries about the genetics of anthrax. In response to concerns from scientists and members of the government, the FBI has asked a panel of independent experts from the National Academy of Sciences to review the scientific findings in the case. The panel will review the accuracy of the genetic studies, the procedures that the FBI used to keep anthrax samples from contaminating each other, and the question of whether the four key mutations in the attack anthrax could also be found in unrelated strains of the bacteria.

The questions raised by the Amerithrax case go beyond the guilt or innocence of one suspect, important though that is. Also at stake is the accuracy and usefulness of microbial forensics, which has great potential for investigating crimes involving biological weapons. Based on the work done in the Amerithrax case, scientists in fields such as molecular biology and genetics are working with the FBI to research the use of mutations to trace strains of infectious disease bacteria back to their source. The methods used in the FBI laboratory could be of great help in investigating medical crimes and biological attacks, but only if those methods are found to be sound and reliable.

Further research is needed before scientific experts can be sure that mutations in bacteria and viruses are completely accurate as a way of identifying a particular strain of a disease organism. If the same mutation can occur more than once in widely separated samples of a given organism, for example, mutations may prove to be less reliable as evidence than scientists now think. On the other hand, if microbial forensics is widely accepted as a valuable tool, the federal government may be called on to create a "library" of DNA sequences for all microbes—bacteria, viruses, and fungi—that could be used as weapons. It may also be necessary to establish new laboratories for the highly specialized work of analyzing microbial DNA, and to train law enforcement and public health agencies in the proper collection and handling of microbial evidence.

Questioning and testing, looking for holes in each new theory or technique, and presenting discoveries to other experts for their review—these are vital aspects of the scientific method. They are the tools by which science moves forward. No area of science has benefited more from new developments than medical and biological forensics, an aspect of forensic science that can save lives as well as solve mysteries.

▼ GLOSSARY

antemortem before death

autopsy a medical examination performed on a body to find the cause of death; a forensic autopsy also tries to establish the time and manner of death

chain of custody a written or digital record of the history of each piece of evidence, from crime scene to trial, with information about everyone who has handled the evidence and why

coroner the public official responsible for determining cause of death; the position does not require medical training

decedent a dead person

decomposition the process of decay and tissue breakdown that happens after death because of the action of bacteria

DNA deoxyribonucleic acid, the substance that contains each individual's genetic code and is found in blood, saliva, and other fluids and tissues of the body

DNA typing the use of DNA to identify individuals; DNA typing may also match a person to a piece of evidence or establish a relationship between two individuals

exhumation the opening of a grave to allow access to a buried body for purposes of forensic examination

fatalities deaths of persons

forensic science the use of scientific knowledge or methods to investigate crimes, identify suspects, and try criminal cases in court

forensics in general, debate or review of any question of fact relating to the law; often used to refer to forensic science

homicide murder

medical examiner (**ME**) a public official responsible for determining cause of death; the position requires medical training

microbial forensics the investigative technique that tracks the origin and development of microbes, or microscopically small organisms, such as those that cause disease

morgue a special medical facility, usually part of a hospital or forensic lab, where bodies are stored and autopsies take place

odontology the study of teeth and dental work; forensic odontology is the use of teeth to identify the dead

pathologist a physician who specializes in the study of illness and death, especially in determining the cause of death

postmortem after death

SANE sexual assault nurse examiner, a nurse specially trained in examining victims of sexual assault and collecting evidence that meets forensic standards for use in court

serology the branch of medical and forensic science that deals with blood

taphonomy the study of the physical changes in a body after death

toxicology the branch of medical, environmental, and forensic science that deals with drugs, poisons, and harmful substances

toxins substances that are poisonous to living organisms; many toxins are poisonous only to certain living things, or only in certain doses

▼ FIND OUT MORE

FURTHER READING

Adelman, Howard. *Forensic Medicine.* New York: Chelsea House, 2006.

Auden, Scott. *Medical Mysteries: Science Researches Conditions from Bizarre to Deadly.* Washington, DC: National Geographic, 2008.

Brezina, Corona. *Careers as a Medical Examiner.* New York: Rosen, 2008.

Ferllini, Roxana. *Silent Witness.* Buffalo, NY: Firefly Books, 2002.

Funkhluser, John. *Forensic Science for High School Students.* Dubuque, IA: Kendall Hunt, 2005.

Innes, Brian. *DNA and Body Evidence.* Armonk, NY: Sharpe, 2007.

Jeffrey, Gary. *Autopsies: Pathologists at Work.* New York: Rosen, 2008.

Walker, Maryalice. *Pathology.* Broomall, PA: Mason Crest, 2005.

WEBSITES

www.forensicmed.co.uk

The British site Forensic Medicine for Medical Students offers information on such topics as autopsies, head injuries, careers in forensic medicine, and more.

http://health.discovery.com/fansites/drg/drg-fansite.html

The companion site to the show "Dr. G.: Medical Examiner" profiles the work of a California medical examiner, with examples of her cases.

http://thename.org

The website of the National Organization of Medical Examiners (NAME) includes a FAQ page that answers questions about the work, education, and career opportunities of medical examiners and pathologists.

www.theforensicnurse.com/ForensicNursingDefined.cfm
www.iafn.org

The websites of The Forensic Nurse and the International Association of Forensic Nurses (IAFN) answer the question "What Is a Forensic Nurse?" Each site gives an overview of forensic nurses' training, careers, and responsibilities.

www.fbi.gov/anthrax/amerithraxlinks.htm

The FBI's Amerithrax Investigation web page has information about the 2001 anthrax case, which involved the transmission of deadly spores through the U.S. mail.

www.aafs.org/yfsf/index.htm

The website of the American Academy of Forensic
Sciences (AAFS) features the Young Forensic
Scientists Forum (YFSF), with information on
careers in forensics. The site also links to other
Internet resources.

www.crimezzz.net/forensic_history/index.htm

The Crimeline page offers a brief timeline of
developments in forensic science from prehistory
to the present.

www.forensicmag.com

The website of *Forensic Magazine* features case
studies and news about developments in forensic
science, including articles about recovery and
investigation work after major disasters.

▼ BIBLIOGRAPHY

The author found these books and articles especially helpful when researching this volume.

Cohle, Stephen, and Tobin Buhk. *Cause of Death: Forensic Files of a Medical Examiner.* Amherst, NY: Prometheus Books, 2007.

"Forensic Dentistry Key in Identifying Victims of Tsunamis, Other Disasters." *Science Daily*, April 6, 2005, online at www.sciencedaily.com/releases/2005/03/050326005336.htm

Fuller, Thomas. "Using Scientific Tools in an International War on Fake Drugs." *New York Times*, July 20, 2009, online at www.nytimes.com/2009/07/21/science/21coun.html

Grady, Denise. "Autopsies of War Dead Reveal Ways to Save Others." *New York Times*, May 25, 2009, online at www.nytimes.com/2009/05/26/health/26autopsy.html

James, Stuart H., and Jon J. Nordby. *Forensic Science: An Introduction to Scientific and Investigative Techniques.* 2nd edition. Boca Raton, FL: Taylor & Francis, 2005.

Mann, Robert. *Forensic Detective.* New York: Ballantine, 2006.

Marshall, Andrew. "Prescription for Murder."
Smithsonian, October 2009, 32.

Mintz, Jessica. "Swine Flu—Digital Detectives." *U.S.
News & World Report*, April 29, 2009, online at
www.usnews.com/science/articles/2009/04/29/
swine-flu-digital-detectives.html

Oxenham, Marc, editor. *Forensic Approaches to Death,
Disaster, and Abuse.* Bowen Hills: Australian
Academic Press, 2008.

Page, Douglas. "Dead Reckoning. *Forensic Magazine*,
Summer 2004. Online at www.forensicmag.com/
articles.asp?pid=9

Payne-James, Jason. *Forensic Medicine: Clinical and
Pathological Aspects.* Cambridge, UK: Greenwich
Medical Media, 2003.

Temple, John. *Deadhouse: Life in a Coroner's Office.*
Jackson: University Press of Mississippi, 2005.

Timmermans, Stefan. *Postmortem: How Medical
Examiners Explain Suspicious Deaths.* Chicago:
University of Chicago Press, 2006.

Zugibe, Frederick, and David Carroll. *Dissecting
Death: Secrets of a Medical Examiner.* New York:
Broadway Books, 2005.

▼ INDEX

▼ ABOUT THE AUTHOR

REBECCA STEFOFF is the author of many books on scientific subjects for young readers. In addition to writing previous volumes in the Forensic Science Investigated series, she has explored the world of evolutionary biology in Marshall Cavendish's Family Trees series; she also wrote *Robot* and *Camera* for Marshall Cavendish's Great Inventions series. After publishing *Charles Darwin and the Evolution Revolution* (Oxford University Press, 1996), she appeared in the *A&E Biography* program on Darwin and his work. Stefoff lives in Portland, Oregon. You can learn more about her books for young readers at **www.rebeccastefoff.com**.